i

c

o

p

e

For more information, find CCM at:

http://copingmechanisms.net

THE

YELLOW

HOUSE

—

CHIWAN

CHOI

i chose poetry
over honesty
then lived this unremarkable life.

there were times
when i wanted to share
all the secrets
that i held on to,

but i was so afraid
that i'd once again
be taken to a new land
with road signs
i couldn't understand

and start over,
even as time was running out,
all of us getting older,
my family and lovers and friends,

the search for the house
of my dreams haunted,
the one that i first saw
as a child
yellow in the winter
of a place called home.

i have tried so hard
to not care
because that's how i was taught
you become a man.

but last night on the roof
we waited for the moon to rise
above los angeles and counted the planes
lined up on the horizon and waiting too,
each waiting for its turn

to land, and i looked
across the courtyard
at the yellow building with the pool
and the big room with space enough
that had made me want a family of my own.

i unraveled until i was speechless,
until i couldn't even tell lies.

this is stupid and emotional
and not poetic at all,
but life is so weird and beautiful
and i can't tell whether it's slipping away

or if it's drowning me.
i can't get out of bed
and if there was skin next to me
i would bury all the feelings in it
to some 80s soundtrack
like a non-stop loop
of the best of the church.

look.

it's just a tuesday morning
and it will be afternoon
and there will be something that makes me laugh,
maybe something my mother says,
and i'll catch her staring at my face

wondering when i became so old,
hiding her own secrets
like how she stays up at night
afraid of the end

wondering if this entire journey
was just to find the proper way
to say goodbye to love.

*

while my parents were gone
i hid in the bush in front of our house
while the other boys lured all the stray dogs
up our driveway and into our back yard

when there were enough
of the dogs
of us
we chased them out

and i jumped out of the bush
with a broomstick
and swung it at the dogs' legs
tripping them
making them fly
tumble
break
down the steep driveway

i stood there and watched
as the dogs lifted themselves up
whimpering
frightened
and limped and ran away

i was 9 and there was something that i wanted
and it was growing inside of me
and there was nothing i could do
to stop

i look up at the hand i am holding
that no longer belongs to mother

we are upstairs
it is dark

and she has a hole in her stomach
i can see through it

and i don't have the words to ask her
if we will meet again

and she only tells me
i need to keep looking
until i see

everything that falls
into place

like water on skin.
i breathe

in the space in the things
you say:

oh—i...

a small hand floating
through the air

like longing.

a mystery
a secret
a memory

repressed on the steps of a house
in Korea that dad built for us.

it was gray   (the building, remembering)
it was white   (the air around it, winter)
it wasn't yellow   (the dream of it, wanting)

there is   crying.

there is   a ghost.

there is   my father.

there is   me.

it is winter.

                         then summer.

it is the beginning   (of self, running)

we touch down on US soil
we are taken to Santa Monica beach
i don't remember having seen the ocean before

there is the touch of sand at the bottom of my feet
i look up at the sun
and suddenly i can't remember my name

a hand pulls at my arm
this is skin on my skin
he wants me to race against him

i tumble into the sand
he pulls away toward the finish line
and stops to tell me to keep running

but i don't rise into the air
and instead watch him cry
as he promises to make me whole

we stood out in the front yard.
i stared at the giant ant hills

in the center divider of our street.
he looked up at the sky

and put his hand on my shoulder.
i turned and tilted my head to face him.

"this is what i want for you," he said.
"to learn to stand in the light and see the storm."

he painted the house yellow.
his son called it canary yellow.

the boy may have been right.
in that house,

they were going to begin a new life.
they planted roses in the front yard.

his wife planted poppy
and told funny stories about opium.

in that house
he started to heal,

although he had to sell his youth
to the ghost in the hallway.

in that house
his wife drank her first beer.

in that canary yellow house,
his son grew up until his bones started to hurt.

in that house the dogs
barked until they died.

in that house
he thanked god

until his son put on his shoes
and left.

it was yellow.
canary yellow in the sun.

once inside
he paced around the large square table
his hands in the pockets of his jeans
that seemed looser than the week before

he wouldn't look up
his eyes roaming over the mess
of paper and books
on the table

i leaned against the kitchen counter
waiting for one of us to speak

waiting for one of us to break

last night i heard the guitar again. i was asleep.
there was pain in my hand to remind me.

*

in the melody, the breaking was faint.
but it was there like this love between a dragonfly and an osprey.

*

as i often do, i cried in the dark, once again close
to learning my name.

*

in the morning, there was a humming from my lips,
how i want to forget—clips of a scene too short to be recorded.

*

this—this makes little sense.
but i am alone heading west, squinting at the sun.

*

my lip are still rough from the burn
of the soup in the small red pot.

*

fracture. that's the word i embrace as night falls,
hoping this is how life begins.

*

full of memories that wrap fingers around ribs.

this is not a memory

this is only a story

this is when i am one

this is not when i am anything

i am just born

i have an older brother

neither of us had a say

this is not a memory

this is not my memory

i have not started remembering

i have not learned to ask what it is to remember

but in this thing that is not a memory

there is a window

there is my brother

he is crying

because he is becoming invisible

he is becoming what fades

this is not a memory

but his blindness

temporary except here

where it's permanent like

all the things we lose like

all the things we try to erase

in his left arm
he holds me tucked like a football

i will remember the smell of his sweat
from working on the construction site
all day

at two and three
there is a growth on the left side of my neck

a homunculus

and this is where my father is focused
his thumb going into his mouth
and being covered in his spit

which he lowers to the growth
and rubs

it will go away, he says over and over,

it will all go away.

the trees blur outside the window as i rest my head against it

the numbers too they fly by caught in midair like thoughts

one eight three zero five last minute goodbyes or until later

the galaxy in your cupped hands still less impossible than the skin
of your fingers

this summer without shirts without god marking translucence
with your sweat

what will we do now what will we say some numbers caught

in space making rain footstep the porch free free free free

each time i change each time you leave under my window

there hands clapping in the storm like peaches like heart in concept

i count light posts and yellow houses
as the song enters its third minute.

for the next 10 seconds
there will be no words.

> *in a yellow house, she listened*
> *to Mahalia Jackson*
>
> *while stitching zippers*
> *on the back of black skirts.*

she sometimes appears
when i am staring at the ceiling.

her face.
it is full of curiosity.

one day, she said,
i will learn as you become.

there is an image in my head
of me lying on my back
on the ground outside the world trade center

it's 1989
and gary's telling us to do that and look up
that the building would look like it was going to fall on me

i remember visualizing it as he spoke
i remember lying there on the ground

but i can't ever remember
what it is that i saw
what it was that took my breath away

here is the world

here is something else like a broken chopstick—

a photo of him standing by a river, a
satchel of arrows on his back,

like a mountain crumbling of loneliness.

i can't remember the last time
my mother told me that she was praying

for our baby to be returned.
faith. it was always her faith.

tonight she sits across me
to watch me eat the soup she has heated up.

my father is on the couch,
his hands resting on his belly,

sounds of guns and explosions coming
from the tv in front of him.

there isn't room enough
in prayer to save both worlds

so she chooses him instead.
and it's no longer Jesus—

her faith directs her to me.
she tells me what she wants

for dad's 80th birthday,
a trip somewhere they haven't seen.

New Zealand, she says,
and i nod because i don't know how to be god

and she loses the words of scripture
when he is dying.

i will promise her these things she asks for
because we weren't born to love

like this.
we were meant to die in war

or hunger.
or loneliness.

*

it starts in one ear
then moves to the other

across my brain
behind my eyes

her voice
the one that never got a chance

she speaks to me
from space

from a life that i thought
was supposed to happen

within reach of my hands
but i have been wrong

about many things.
as a child i sat on the step

that went down into the kitchen
with a book in my hand

learning how to make the words
i couldn't yet read

mean what i needed them to say
and watched my mother

thinking she was cooking
when she was fighting to stay alive

as a woman
married to a family of man

and i told her
that she would live til 250

because i thought
i only had to need for it to be true

i hear her
speaking

alive.

ashes of a birth misdirected, speak to me as

winter embraces and fingers trace the outline

of light like a rough face dimpled by shame.

in my dreams i caught the arrows and other storms

hoping to find her exhales.

but there were only beasts sheltered in the folds of this wind.

speak to me, daughter.

there has been too much silence.

there has been too much forgetting.

i dream of this house crumbling to dust
god standing there ready to spit on it
and begin to mold it again into a shape
that holds more than absence

when i breathe there is an echo
frequencies from a cry that let out
five years ago or 45

i have started to hear my name again
and i smile and break and
want to live want to live want to live
even toward this inevitable end

i dream and forget the moment i wake
reaching toward her disappearance
and the doors that have been left open
desperate for a breeze of summer

it is easy to blame the thing my skin wanted.
you are the light and you left
this stubborn house a mess

but you will be back at the way
you came to me when i was a child
and i have to believe these things
because i don't know how else
to push time forward

on the porch
drinking barley tea so my legs won't fail
(that's what mother says)
and, for a moment,
looking at my hand.
it is still.
sometimes it shakes,
trembles.
sometimes it holds
tight
the world.

the floor
is invisible under suitcases and boxes

we are in the process of beginning again
purging

boxing up regrets
and shipping them to a new home

we've been at this for days
i can't even remember

the things
now hidden
that we are saving

my father
walks me
to jesus

he says

                              listen
                              to what he tells you

and i wet my pants
but do as he says

he teaches me
salvation only comes
through pain

so i hammer
at my bones
in my sleep

the abductions
then come
until my language is lost

my mother
tells me
in silence

                    learn to dig
                              the alien soil

                              for sharp fragments
                                   of lives long gone

and to carve
into the surface
of the world

the thing inside
that they tried
to take away

in this new world

she says

it is no longer a heart
it is called a poem

and

you are
arsenal
buried

for the ones to come

this is how
you breathe

this is how
you speak

this is how
you break

and become
unstoppable

this is the same trumpet.
the same piano.

                                        the same pitch of
your voice.

                        this is the same silence
                        hidden in my whisper.

this is loneliness.

this is how much we don't care.

the same curl of your elbow.
            the same loose hair on my sleeve.
this
                              is the same miracle that will kill
us.

            this is the lamp of a night we can't weather.
                  this is saying it out loud.

            the same confusion.

this is the guitar.
the same chords.

the same floor we sprawled upon the same route we can no longer trace.

this is my father.

the same mother.

the same eulogy.

                                                  the same
deflection.

this is the quiet lunch with soup too hot.
the same untrained eye.
the same key.

this the skin before the touch from the tip of a tongue and a breeze
carrying last night's rain through

                                                      the rising sun.

i run home from school
and cry as my mother sits at

her sewing machine,
mahalia jackson on her tape deck

humming as i move past her
into my room. she walks in

and sits on my brother's bed,
robert still not home,

and puts her hand on my back
while i sob into my pillow.

why were we moved here, i ask.
why did we leave?

she tells me to turn my back
on the home i have never even known.

you are now almost 15, she says.
you can no longer cry.

in a stranger's music,
i heard my own voice.

      in my voice, i heard my brother
      giving me the keys to his Camaro.

            in that night on that twisty part of Sunset,
            i heard my mother asking me to come home.

in that home i heard my father
falling asleep on the couch.

      in his dream i heard
      a girl's hair flutter in the breeze.

            in the breeze i saw my sister.
            i saw my sister in the breeze.

i forgot what we were laughing about.

they were comparing their sun burned arms.

they looked like those fish sausages from the Korean market.

mom's arm was the reddest, but i kept looking at her unburned parts.

it looks like she is shrinking inside and her skin is too loose.

later i took a photo of her with dad.

i showed it to her.

"this is nice. i don't look so old in this photo," she said.

then we laughed.

i remember what we were laughing about that time.

we head for the waterfalls

falling in and out of sleep
i look out the window into the dark night
and fall in love
with everything
i cannot see

i don't know what time it is
but it's late
and most everyone is asleep
or at least quiet

but my father stands up
from his seat at the very front
and turns to face the rest of us

he is a silhouette
a shadow that i can love
as his shadow arm raises
and his shadow finger points
toward a place
that we are supposed to remember

i make street lights appear on the ceiling
until we can no longer be the same

like the red of a house of bricks from childhood
like the dead rising from the pavement in the rain

the words i wanted to hear were:

your body is a haunted house

so i could close the windows

keep the winter from my dead

but all that is showing

are bones that have frayed

beyond explanation

wrapped in yellow skin burnt on alien landscapes

on the train, we wanted to be watched
by the late night riders.

but i fell asleep in the seat next to her.
it was only for a few seconds.

when i woke up, i wanted to tell her
that i remembered now:

      she'd been reading a book.
      i was counting the flags that continued to flap

            while we prayed
            we had lost the sun.

where am i when she tells me
that there is something wrong

she is not ok

i identify the texture around me
a blue cloth touched by hundreds before

shaped and tinted like mismatching bricks
promising a childhood i could have cherished

outside the window
is the air i must have promised her

when our future was still our witness
and i am hearing the words i typed:

hello. how are you. are you better.

when was it that i stopped expecting
a real answer

i have a hard time letting go of people
so hard that i start losing them the moment

our skins first touch
trying to file into memory how there was sweat

covering hers, mine, yours
just below the length of the sleeve

at nights i lie on my broken shoulder
to say goodbye before i lose my chance

why did we meet this way
why did i learn your name this way

there is something wrong, she says,
i am not ok.

i am not ok.

it's just some typed words appearing on my screen
but in here, so far up in the air,

i hear the words
spoken by every voice i have known

and the ones i haven't
imagining the timbre and drawl

and the way the tongues and lips strangers
wrap around these words

hello. i am not ok.

what is goodbye and when does the utterance begin?
i am here sitting in the air

and i feel alone
without contact

trying to count all the faces
remember all the skin

that i started to love
whose names i learned to say
only as they had already started to leave.

on another sunny day waiting—

the sounds of shoes on pavement break.

i asked her once if she'd seen me cry.

we forget how much we have exposed.

here is the piano again.

soon it will be a guitar.

what was so important, more important

than the dog who chases the wilderness she has not known?

we will learn together to mourn

a life that was never going to change.

we will say "i am yours" and shelter to grieve

the days we have left to count down.

and you find it,
while burning,
the house you were searching for

where you could be born again
on rocks as if you always belonged
in and to the world,

held safely
in hands that harnessed the storms
fingers curled unexpectedly

brown
yellow

that color that was
meant to be life

even after the city is destroyed,
i will touch you on the surface of everything.

48 hours public

valid proof of fare

when did your heart go missing

please, no

la última palabra

but your life

this is when the door opened to a fence

the lights, the lights

the lights that night

you knew the next note that starts the melody

passenger i'm proposing

moving back and the other way

we are souvenirs

waiting for a table in a building made of logs.
there are some things that remain standing through fires
and earthquakes and even wars i suppose.

i am on a bench on the third floor and i can see
my family, my parents and my big brother,
sitting on the second floor on the other side.

today i wanted to ask mom if she was happy
that we were brought here so many years ago.
i also wanted to ask her if she regrets her life

and if she thinks about the day there will be no more
of us, when our line, when their line, dies. but i couldn't.
it wasn't a choice. i just couldn't.

instead i just stood behind her in the cold wind,
holding the binocular in front of her eyes, helping her see
the white mountain goat on up on the rocks,

trying to help her see this small majestic thing
that walks on an impossible edge made of stone.

they watched through the back window of the school bus
as i followed in my 76 monte carlo
we'd salvaged from the junkyard

i waved and turned the wheel to the left
onto the wrong side of the street

my foot pushing down on the gas
as the faces on the windows began to contort

i closed my eyes
as i passed them
heading into oncoming traffic

thinking of the water
touching my feet where the ocean begins
and ends

he mistook Robertson for Robinson
and I thought i heard someone clap behind me.

i turned and looked straight at a young couple,
her head on his shoulder all awkward
because she was so much taller than him.

i blushed.
i put the earphones back on
and listened to guitars.

when i looked out,
there was a yellow apartment building
appearing than gone.

i wanted to feel happy then.
i wanted that so much.

we drive through koreatown
i roll down the window
as the tank stands silently next to us

i stick my head out and look up
at the night sky
smell my childhood tangled
somewhere in the smoke

my city is burning
and the soldiers are yelling at us
to go home

fuck you, we yell

and we laugh
while we fall apart

because there is nothing
for us to do

in the fire that had waited
for so long

my sweet town
always
burning
always

burning

i want to call the city my home,
follow the red lights that move away
from me at nights.

we are the dogs that howl
for the fires that rage
and the body finding rest on the sidewalk.

i want to call the city my home,
the pavement that cracks at the slightest hint of winter.

oh monuments, preserved by neglect,
how you dreamt that one day you'd be the shelter
for the lost masses that were willing to pay with blood.

i want to call you home, city of mine,
even as you shed your skin once again
and pretend you are once more a newborn.

how do we leave
and leave behind

when the flood takes our car
a sun faded red vw bug

into the mouth
of the strange tongue

the first time he fell off the ladder
he washed the dirt off his elbows at the kitchen sink

mother knit another blanket
a christmas gift for an 85 year old woman at her church

at night i came home to the coyote at the door
watching me as i tried to forget my name

he kept falling and there was first too much
then nothing more to clean

he looked up at me from the floor
at the bottom of the stairs

briefly

before rolling away so i couldn't see his face

i stood at the top of the stairs

hesitating

as i tried to hide all of my secrets

he couldn't call to me

and i wouldn't run down to him

because neither of us could measure
the distance between us.

he waits for me to transform
to become an american machine

i am meant to edit him
meant to revise him

dress him in a new skin of copper
that covers the gears and pistons

that smell of our mornings
on gramercy drive

it was of the oil spilling
it was of the grass dying

and for a moment
i imagined i was a wolf

or that half of me was

and i was walking through the snow
with my pack

searching for the place
i marked with my first breath

how many springs had she greeted
in a dress and scuffed boots.

he did too, the opening of arms to hold space.
there on the grass on their sides,

fingertips grazing skin,
sun bright on her curved hip,

the bit of dried skin on his lower lip
threatening to fall off by summer,

they embraced the abductions
that would one day begin anew

whether they stayed or got up and left.
they did one more thing:

they decided it was ok to be
terrified by this desire to love.

today
i returned to her apartment

       the one with the crooked shelves
       and the small fan

and ran my fingers
through the dust on the windowsill

       to feel the burning of steel
       to taste the silence of the dying

i returned to look for myself
on a bed long gone

this morning i had thought of something
from that time in my life

       where i was afraid of discovering
       all that my heart wanted

somewhere between those walls
i can still hear myself crying

       in my sleep, dreaming of something
       that i would lose before i woke

i want to come home to this again
days of being unmade instead of broken

       this is terror and desperation
       i am losing words like that faith that fled long ago

i need you
i need you to tell me how to say goodbye

       to the details that shift shapes like memories
       like faces that lit up a dark March night Los Angeles

1980
and the beginning of loss

       and how all i wanted
       was a moment that would keep me still

she asks if it's possible
to map a body this body

and i think of the terrain
that i can't escape even

if we cross the borders
and oceans over and again

i think of the hollow in the cracked
bones of countless quakes

she asks about the map
that is my body this body

and i look for the place
where i begin

these eyes hanging like
tiny twin stars above the mountains

that burned out before
i even knew i was born

the wet street that runs
through my elbow healed

that carries my brother
who pedals away from me

the south, my knees
swollen and pulsing

burning fires trailing down
to my feet

at the northern tip this scar
on my forehead left

from the closing off
of the blood inside

hiding the curse my father
left for me before work

and at the end of a two lane highway
too short to wrap around a life that begins

my hands, my hands, fists
pounding on the metal slab

until i can't feel
their emptiness

she asks is your body this body
a map, cartographer

and i don't know how to reach
for my heart having

forgotten long ago
what you call that road you took

to a place finally quiet enough
to lose everything

that place that reminded you

of home enough to make you run

how you still hold the soil
from its ground

under your nails
years and hours after

you couldn't leave anymore

we are speaking of love and of empty bottles by square windows
and bare legs that push for speed and how we are okay
we are okay and we are speaking of falling through the people
we want to own and how elbows bend around yellow poles
and numbers that tease you by ending in a 3

and we are speaking of blindness and the tree
we have anchored our lives to and how I am living
in a new neighborhood even though I haven't moved
and the taste of fingers running through hair

and we are speaking through moments of open doors
and of the water sitting still on the counter and of love
and the rain that falls on a green umbrella
on an otherwise forgettable afternoon in March.

before we began again,
we held each other's face.

she said something about cigarettes.
i mistook Sunday for Saturday.

what happens when we're old, he asked,
when we're old and decrepit?

her lower lip was shiny with his spit.
this, she said. this.

we bit each other until we bled.

some time before the night began.

we stood on our fifth floor balcony
months after she was gone

hands on the black railing
covered in downtown dust

and across the courtyard at the large windows
of an empty apartment

we looked in trying to see
a life begin again.

tell me again of the afternoon in the shade of a small tree we buried our teeth in each others lips as next to us an ancient stone sat in silent elevation. tell me again before the doors close the next stop of this nameless train filled with music from a present that peeks its head into my line of vision when i am not ready. tell me again and tell me again of that life underground that is too much to ask. tell me tell me tell me where we used to be before the lemons fell from the tree by your feet while you touched your cheek with one hand. how does love work in our lives and why does it never fail to break the skeleton within us.

my mother excitedly urges us
to join her on the rooftop

the moon, she says, the moon is huge tonight.
the biggest of the year.

i ask her
when she first embraced magic

and she reaches for her keys
and shakes her head at father

his jaws clenched tight
on the couch in front of the tv

what is magic when there is faith, she says

on the rooftop
she embraces the light
and lends me her faith

and i say
no this needs to be magic

and i say
no this needs to be time

in the sun
another 110 degree summer

we lose our shoes and our shirts
roam the streets with out machetes
hunting dinosaurs

my father yells at me
because i am sucking juice
out of a grapefruit i have
ripped from our tree

you're going to lose your teeth, he says
chasing me with a stick

i run to my cousin Diana
who i pretend is my sister

she is now in Hawaii
studying how our languages work
and looking for ways to run and hide
from her own parents
who are dying and unreasonable

i have kept my teeth
even while losing my future

last week i sat across my mother
as she sliced oranges

and i put a slice in my mouth
the peel sticking out like a boxer's mouthpiece

and she laughed
and i laughed

and my father
on the couch watching tom cruise on tv
laughed too
his teeth long gone.

they told me to sit on the edge of their bed.
fix him, she said to him.

give me your foot, he said to me.
i straightened my leg and held my breath

as he put his hands on my left foot and gripped
and she watched as i held my breath

as i grimaced while he broke me
to fix me again

he called to us before the building was torn down.

it's a shame, he said.

i nodded because i was too tired to not.

but now i am looking at white birds painted on a wall
in a different part of a town too big to ever escape

and i am angry because they are not birds at all,
but careless n's in white.

let them tear it down, tear it all down.

at least we'll have the shattered walls for a while.
these memories—the cement on our feet

that keep us anchored to the bottom of the lake,
drowning, silent,

hidden in something transparent.

what comes after this moment
after my fingers lose contact

       from the back of her hand?
       it is winter outside

              because the silence tells me
              and i lose track of day and night

my mother, who is 3000 miles away,
wants to plan a future trip

       that will hold off an unbearable loneliness
       and all i can do is nod

              back to the hand
              that becomes more familiar

invisible each day—
like the sound of Phillip Glass's imagination

       caught between leaving
       and being left behind

              what is this life where i kill
              before a life can be taken away from me

in a city that can't know my name
or the texture thick like sugar

       i once told a stranger next to me
       that i knew something that matters

but it was a mistake
born of wanting

i am on another bus
on another night

through the space that we hold between us
that grows, unrepentant,

each time
we make a decision to live.

in the morning i watch a city that no longer recognizes itself.
there is a woman adjusting the purse strap on her left shoulder.
i snap a photo of her as she looks up.

these city blocks are images of angles
that promise recognition from a past that i've had
or from a future i'm supposed to embrace.

walking through a DTLA morning
backed by a Sigur Rós soundtrack—
this is how you break your own heart.

i take one more picture but it comes out all wrong.
instead of shadows, there are words
and focus once more is thrown off by sentiment.

there was the day
we looked up at the sky together

and saw the same invasion
the same lights

and you were
what i imagine proud

we are running out of time
in our knowing of each other

for me to say
that i need you to be

ashamed of nothing
that i carry

that i need you to show me
a future of fire

what color am i, father?

they took him
from one land to another
and broke him until
his mouth would release
the word home.

at nights
from his room
he tried to catch the sky
in its act of darkening
through his window peeking—
one day I-he would embrace
the way secrets
kept from loved ones
keep us alive—

what was it to want
to desire
without the grasp of familiar walls
there was only the boy
and the life after the first abduction
that forced upon him a new language
dressed in the fabric of choice.

one summer
he no longer could walk
and he looked up at the fan spinning
above him
remembering the way Jesus laughed
at the shape of his face

and in this stillness
brought by pain
he wanted only to breathe
into a skin like his skin
each breath   *like digging*
                      like a life in circle
                      like a burial.

tonight i only expect the clenched fists and teeth unwashed biting down in silence

because this is my life right now trying to disappear in the footsteps of strangers and searching for a spot on a floor flat enough to call home

but somewhere in the unfolding of her elbow as she spoke of the lies that kept her alive even after losing her brother at his ninth month to remnants of agent orange or personal guilt

somewhere in the way her finger pointed toward an unexpected sweet darkness

i once again wanted to know the secret behind and beyond our names

we stare at each other's hands.
yellow paint stains us both.
we shrug and laugh.

it's Monday morning
and Dad and i are together.

just like he has done,
i've lived my life believing
in a beyond

in a place we can sit around a table
and eat pork dumplings all day.

and just like him,
i have learned there's only this,
sharing the stains of a life so short,

laughing at the miracle of it.

the language you began to utter
in the womb to one day let you
love and fear god hidden in the falling
of a petal like your future
now burning toward its end

this is the language you lose to speak
words that you were never supposed to know
words that will go on to scar your tongue
because your father believed in penance
and he wanted you to be saved

you are now 46 and you are in ways still alive
but he hasn't read a single one of these sentences
you've spoken and it has been freedom
to not be heard and it has been a death in silence

what was supposed to happen when by chance
you found the house that had haunted your life
the house yellow in a sun you couldn't name
enter take space live and allow yourself to make plans
or if you were meant to stand outside and watch
it burn while you learned to pray in this forced
language for the storm that will extinguish you

you are listening to the end
of the new frank ocean album
and the music is what you always wished
the end of your life to sound like
not the words because you've had too much
of language that you don't belong to

just the music for the final breaths

final pages final turns around the moon the sun
around the fire we built together on the beach
around our dead around our taken around the bones
that shiver at the touch of lips on bare shoulders
around the final wanting around our breaking
around our breaking around our breaking

there is a song again
because i am trying to hide

between two conflicting notes.
it is loud and the sun is hot

like what used to be called home.
in time, i will regret the way my hand

trembled, perhaps shook.
sometimes i mistake the keyboard

for the plucking of guitar strings
and blame my father because he is dying.

the unsteadiness of my desire is what
blurred the outline of our house,

the one before the one that was painted
yellow for hoping, the lines that i tried

to section and beg into shape
using small words with hard sounds

guitar plucks
keyboard

                    some people want to die
                        so they can be free

fingers invisible like the wind warm
my arms holding in the air

                                        wilting
                                        writing
                                        etching
                                        carving
                                        a word shaped anger

to be a punctuation
for once
of my own making.

                            *

my mother smiles across the table
and i turn up the music louder

and there is that point
where love is replaced by the silence

of the drowning of need

and that point loud enough to mishear the words
for a second singing

                        so i want to die so they can be free
                        is that right because it feels right

the making of this space between us
the width of a brown wooden table

into my place of unfocus
                                unravel

                                    unveil

                                        unwant

unwanting

not to remember
not to honor
not to hold the weight of skin
in prayer
in offering
in sacrifice

*

this is the outline of my house faded
this is the outline of daughter aging in space

this is the giving up of trying to save us
this the horizon and the summer that's coming

this:mother as fable of a woman in process

this:father as the story of the thief of voices

this:brother as a blueprint of a column at the square

this:death as freedom
                    (is it *what if i die so they can be free?*)

this:memory as erasure

this:portrait of a family as lines that once existed

this:poet as the note that was reached before the loss of hearing

trying to connect dots that go beyond my apartment walls,
beyond the familiarities in my parents' faces,
beyond oxygen trapped in a yellow hue.

trying to connect to the secret i couldn't retrieve
from the alley behind our house in Seoul,
the secret whispered on the foot of the steps by a ghost,

to that face turning from me when i was lost in the halls of a
Brazilian hotel.
i'm trying to remember the name of the one that calls for me over
and over
from somewhere close to the birth of this light.

i know the answer to everything is there in the sound
that will be made when i recognize her face, in darkness,
in eternity, about the reasons i have broken, about where it was

that i was supposed to wait, calculating the wrong side of this
triangle
that keeps spinning around me on one of those days in which
i want to walk up and down a fire escape until the sun dies.

straight down the middle lane of this highway
yellow building yellow free summer day and the angle of a broken arm
and touching the underside of the leaf with the tip of one trembling finger.

in the back seat, we became invisible.
or that's what we told ourselves,
not wanting to admit that nobody ever saw us.

hear this:

all we can do is keep breathing.
this was skin before the touch from the tip of a tongue
and the breeze that lifted last night's rain through the rising sun.

once upon a time i wrote my life out while you slept and gathered my family of lovers and blood

once upon a time i burned my life into ashes and watched the train carry my erasure to the north

once upon a time
my life existed
only in your memory
transformed each day
by your longing

once upon a time this is what i wished:

looking for blame in the dirt of my body like seeds sprouting promises of life

and i was thinking about the air we carry with us, still in the shape of the house that we were born into, the house in which parts of us broke beyond repair. the walls are gone and not gone, still there like the smell of my grandmother's hair on my pillow from the one time she visited us here. and to breathe is a haunting.

a house without walls
this air around us that we carry
what it means to carry desire
for something that is not this moment
how that thing that kills us keeps us alive
maybe home is not where wanting ends

what am i saying?

it's the desert.

i am trying to write about the desert,
but i can only speak of thirst.

why do i lose everything everything i am supposed to hold?

i am looking up now at the sky. in the darkness there is an absence.
she was here. the dragon.

and there was a dragon because i say there was.

i chased the crows
until i was standing alone on train tracks.

how dark it was that night.
but i kept believing as I shivered

in my well worn t-shirt
that i would one day catch their cries.

there is no moon

only this body

it breaks in ways
that don't matter

but you
still

hold the fragments
in your hands

what would the people of science
the physicists and poets
say about your voice
that knows how to travel
between two galaxies
between two universes
between two lives that can't
hold space together
like children in love

and if you are a star
and you are the light that i see
through the din of aging neighbors
and the relentless summer rain
how long ago did you expire?

you make me believe
that what was meant for us
is this life of ghosts
and traveling through time
to learn to long over and over

the abductions
broke me
broke all of us
and taught us
how much breathing
is chained to loss
how surviving is
for fools
who can't put down
faith

tonight the moon
is the moon
and another cycle beginning

here i am
supine
you dancing on the yellow walls
that hold my bones inside
washing me with tears and blood
while i learn again
how to say thank you

and you make me want
to hold the sky
in my hands that are fracturing
until i want to call it blue
in the moment like this one where
my skin loses its boundaries
and all i want
is to live.

the thing you didn't know
is that they age even
after they're gone

they find a sun of their own
and run and fall and breathe

hold their hands against the current
of a cold river

but for the first time
you spoke the dark out loud:

walking through a department store
i saw a girl standing behind a counter
selling something, jewelry perhaps.

she had her head down
standing straight

i am standing in front of her

i say, you are beautiful.
she says, you are beautiful too.

in dreams
you can see a face through hair that hangs down
in front of it like childhood waterfalls

even months later
you will remember remembering
the light caught on her cheeks

repeat the details to yourself while
riding a bus to a smoky bar
how she must have been 15.

(your wife's arm still wrapping around you
as it did that night you dreamt,
as your body shook to let out your cries)

the tears that wouldn't stop
as you say, i remember it all.

*

mom asks me about loneliness, mine,
and i say i am 15 and i am not lonely even if i'm alone

curling up into my body raging against itself into
an unprepared manhood to hide

because my father would anger
in hearing me speak weakness

i want to say that mom asked me what i meant by it,
had asked me to show her the interiors

but all i conjure is her silence, maybe nodding,
her eyes on something less unexplainable than her son.

i am missing something, i tell her,
i always feel like i'm missing someone.

there is silence—there always is
between us, mother and son

(by silence i mean you hear things
like breaths being taken like someone in the act of being alive)

two years before you, she says,
there was a girl.

taken.
gone.

what was her name, i ask.

another word that we chose to forget, she says.

*

the echoes hollow hanging on sheers
breathing at windows long blinded with neglect

and the counters that caught darkness
like open palms in the falling ash

made me believe that i had found home too late

what do you call footsteps taken after the end
of the only journey you've known and what
you've searched for was always just emptiness
or that which had gone

but in a moment walking through the air
wrapped lonely on my skin

i mistook the creak of a floorboard
for my mother's hand on my back

urging me to breathe

the two notes repeating on the piano
from somewhere down the street until they became
te amo engraved into my chest

with my fingers touching the carving of those words
i am learning to embrace the weight of each absence
and how maybe i was always the dream i was

running toward and the rooms are the spaces
that my bones have kept safe inside me
i am the yellow house that i thought was empty

but it is filled with the voices the songs the longing
of my ghosts the ones i thought i lost in my chase
for the life i wanted

daughter
sister
all the dogs
soon my mother
father too
brother one day
and wife

here i am
the end
and i need to find
the way
to rejoice
because i am the house

i am the house

                    amen

i am the house
                    amen

i am the yellow house
                    amen

i am the house
haunted

and faith looks like
letting go of the ghosts
that will never leave your body

i am the yellow
house
of ghosts.

only when it's dark
we can ask
what is fragile—

this bone in my right hand
this ankle that wants to turn
this wall on which i rest my hand

is fragile
the way he holds his avocado sandwich
with two hands
covered in brown spots

how fragile
is this word
i place on this page
only to delete it for its sound
that will not conform

if i was fragile
if i could forever be in the process of breaking
would my hands be enough

to catch salvation
falling
from the sparrow's
impossible grasp

daughter
i prayed instead
when my body told me
to run because my legs
were breaking and i was
afraid of the pain
but i was wrong and i lost you
before the end of grace

i have replaced god
with longing
and i am learning to speak
to birds and the lavender
to ask them to help me chart the stars

i started this story
about the yellow house
to tell you that there was a life
i had wanted so badly

then i thought
'this is where i die'
because that's what it means to want

i am told
that there are other ways
i can be a father

how do i tell them
it was never about giving
myself a name

i just wanted

to speak yours

but what if i could be wrong
one more time
and the yellow house is not
my broken body
nor the hollow that holds me
in burial

daughter
what if my desire
was always your way
of guiding me
to the place where
you learned to cherish your life

last night's rain is gone
and a song plays somewhere not far
and carries down my street.

the melody paralyzes me
and i remember that moment
in which i promised
i'd won
we'd both won
while i slept for the first time
in years.

and i remember colors
some years later
black and red and green
i think
those different colored lines on the floor
guiding us through the halls
of the LA county emergency

hope

        is spelled like

                                knife

like the one my father
put in my hand
while i stood shaking
on redondo pier
as he showed me how to filet
a mackerel without crying

where are the lessons of past nights this morning
when the tears come through the bones

like the sun through the trees
because it is my skin
that slices open.
that's how hope is:

>   your father's hand on your shoulder
>   when he tells you god
>   will care.

i want to call my daughter's name
but memory has replaced the letters with blank spaces—
how many syllables were
going to bring happiness?

alone in an unwelcome light
standing among the boxes that we are carrying
to another home.

you whose name i have lost:

i have for so long
believed i was the monster
at the center of my family
of my love
of everything that breaks
of us

but i am tired
i want to put this anger down
and the hope too
that keeps returning unwanted
and run through the forest
toward the echo
that sounds like my name

being called
from the yellow house
standing weathered
in a field of lavender.

Chiwan Choi is the author of 3 collections of poetry, *The Flood* (Tía Chucha Press, 2010), *Abductions* (Writ Large Press, 2012), and *The Yellow House* (CCM, 2017). He wrote, presented, and destroyed the novel Ghostmaker throughout the course of 2015. Chiwan is a partner at Writ Large Press, a downtown Los Angeles based indie publisher, focused on using literary arts to resist, disrupt, and transgress.

OFFICIAL

CCM ◐

GET OUT OF JAIL
✳ VOUCHER ✳

- -

Tear this out.
Skip that social event.
It's okay.
You don't have to go if you don't want to. Pick up
the book you just bought. Open to the first page.
You'll thank us by the third paragraph.

If friends ask why you were a no-show, show them
this voucher.
You'll be fine.

- -

We're coping.

◐

CPSIA information can be obtained
at www.ICGtesting.com
Printed in the USA
LVOW03s1419040417
529569LV00001B/17/P